THE THRIVING ACCOUNTING PRACTICE

IAN MORGAN

Copyright © 2024 Ian Morgan

All rights reserved.

ISBN: 9798324385149

CONTENTS

	Acknowledgments	i
1	Introduction	1
2	Obtaining financial control	Pg 4
3	A team of A players	Pg 9
4	The "sat-nav" sales process	Pg 17
5	Effective client reviews	Pg 23
6	Being everything to everyone	Pg 26
7	Having financial clarity	Pg 28
8	Creating financial freedom	Pg 30
9	Next steps	Pg 35
10	About the author	Pg 38

ACKNOWLEDGEMENTS

I can't take all the glory.

There became a stage back in 2019, where I had reached the peak, I was capable of.

I finally allowed Sam (my wife) to run the business in her way to see if we could remove some of the final stresses that still remained.

Sam brought a new level of organisation, structure, and a process-driven business, which built great foundations that allowed us to grow to new levels. I've found a way of complimenting my skills with Sam's and together we achieve great things in our business and personal lives. I couldn't and nor would I want to do it without her.

Although Sam firmly remains in the background as she does not enjoy the spotlight, she is definitely a fundamental part of our practice and our personal lives being successful, thank you, Sam.

Also, thanks to my children, Kieran, Chloe, Ellie and Lily for putting up with my late nights, my grumpiness and my constant drive to improve.

Thanks for all of your support, I love you all.

1 INTRODUCTION

When you start out as a practice owner (or any business owner for that fact) you simply need to make sales. It annoys me that successful people say "if I started again I'd niche from day one, I'd say no to any client that wasn't perfect or some other highly selective approach". I just don't think it's true. You'd like it to be true but the reality, let's face it, is that when you just start out you have got bills to pay and regular income of any kind is what you want so you can keep paying those bills and keep a roof over your head.

However, as you grow to higher levels of sales, usually somewhere above £100k, an issue arrives. In fact, many issues start to emerge, but in my opinion, a big issue that arrives, is that you can no longer do this on your own. You need some form of help and normally you end up leaving it longer and longer (just like I did) when what you need is help right now.

Now, there are various mistakes that happen here, such as hiring the wrong person, hiring someone with the wrong skills, not training them correctly, hiring family and friends, getting the wrong character, not onboarding them successfully, and so much more. I, however, want to focus on one particular issue. That issue is that now all of a sudden you have to take a hit to your profits. At least in the short term while you get the new hire up to speed.

You reflect and you're not sure if you should do this but after another evening (or two or three) of burning the midnight oil you decide to proceed with the hire, as you simply can't go on like you are anymore, besides, there aren't any more hours available each week anyway!

This cycle carries on for some time. With a lack of documented processes, a degree of, possibly a large amount, work you probably shouldn't be doing for a number of clients that you don't want to work with! Yet more and more enquiries keep coming so, what choice do you have?

Then one day, you have a bit of a meltdown. Well, when I say a bit! You realise that with all the hours you are working and the small amount of profit you are making it would be illegal to pay a human being what you are getting paid. If that was a member of staff for any organisation apart from their own, you'd be in court for human rights breaches and exploitation!

Something had to change. This business was meant to be about having more control, having more free time, and having more money. That is definitely not the case. In fact, it's the complete opposite. Clients now have all the control and you keep on taking on more and more of them. Free time, the only time that exists is work. Where possible you manage to squeeze in ten minutes for food, I'd say a meal but hey! And time for sleep, that's for wimps, isn't it? As for money, well, that comes later, doesn't it? You know they say battle through the hard times, and you'll reach the good times. Surely my luck will change soon! Won't it?

Now don't worry. You aren't alone. I've been here myself and I've seen many others there too. The very fact you are recognising the issues is HUGE. So many people don't recognise them and failure is often not far away.

There are ways to fix this and more often than not you already know what they are but you are so caught up in the weeds that you don't know where to start. You could think your way out of it but where do you find time to think?

Well, today is the day you realise you NEED to apply everything you already know directly to your practice. But where do you start? This book is here to help.

> You are not alone. Many business owners get stuck simply just surviving. Working too many hours and earning just enough to pay the basic bills. Today is the day you really start your path to financial freedom.

2 OBTAINING FINANCIAL CONTROL

So, you have arrived at this time in your practice where, when people ask how it's going you have a stock response. It's really busy! Now that isn't a lie, is it?! It's not the truth either though if you are being honest with yourself!

It's the one truth that will make people think everything is going great. The real problem here, however, is that you are lying to yourself!

And that is dangerous!

If you don't realise and accept you have a problem, then how is it ever going to get fixed?

So firstly, you must accept as soon as you can, ideally right now, that you have a financial performance issue in your business. You may have other issues too but let's face it, financial performance is the big one. The first and foremost function of a business is to make money. If you can't do that then it leads to more problems.

Not enough clients = a money issue.

If you had more money, then you could do much more marketing, maybe even outsource it and get more clients.

Can't find staff = a money issue.

If you made more money, then that would mean you could pay better salaries and then you'd be able to find staff.

The computer is too slow = a money issue.

If you made more money you could invest in a new higher-spec computer that runs super-fast without issues.

Now there are obviously other issues that exist and I'm not saying money is everything but it is where it starts. I've never found an issue yet that having more money makes it a harder issue to solve.

Let me just say that again... I've never found an issue yet that having more money makes it a harder issue to solve.

So, if your business cannot make money, or at least enough money for you to live a thriving lifestyle then why do what you do?

Just think about this for a moment.

If you ran a job advert for your job it would look something like this...

> **Job description**
>
> Head of sales, marketing, finance, customer service, HR, operations, admin, IT and everything else. Need to be an all-rounder.
>
> Can't ever get tired, need to be happy at all times and set an example to everyone else.
>
> **Hours of work**
>
> 5am to 11pm 7 days per week plus overtime when possible.
>
> **Rate of pay**
>
> Maxes out at £2 an hour if you can keep to the core hours. Goes down from there if you work more.

Now, who in their right mind would even apply for that job? You would have to be mad, right?

Yet I've done that job, I bet you have too! Or even you are doing that job right now!

And I know loads of other accounting practice owners doing it right now too! So you aren't alone. In fact, you could argue you are bang average! Is that why you started this accounting practice though? To be bang average! I doubt it.

The great news is that it doesn't have to be that way. What you want is financial freedom! It's what every entrepreneur wants. But that is the destination. There are some steps you have to go through to get there. The first of those is financial control. I know you must be thinking I'm mad right. Here is a book from an accountant for accountants and in chapter one he has the cheek to start with financial control! I know it sounds crazy and it did to me when I decided what the first step was when looking back on how I transformed my practice. The truth is though I lacked financial control. It was embarrassing but it was true. So even if it's just for a laugh just read on and entertain my thoughts.

So, what is financial control?

As accountants, we should know this better than anyone else. We often do, but rarely do we apply those principles to our own practice.

It's the same as the builder who builds great extensions for their clients. Yet you visit their house and it's almost falling apart. As accountants we aren't as different as you may think.

However, as we already know, accounting is the language of business, and we should be fluent. So, let's firstly get your own house in order and ensure you have financial control.

Now in my view, financial control is a great finance function for your practice that keeps the bookkeeping regular (daily is best) and accurate, where you report on your own performance at least every month preparing a management report versus your budget, and you have a cash flow forecast for at least the next 3 months.

That really shouldn't be that difficult. We already have the tools; we just need to put it into practice.

The truth is most businesses fail and they fail because of a lack of investment in the finance function. You know this already and yet you likely have the weakest accounting function of all your clients!

> 81% of businesses fail within the first five years. Of those that make it beyond, 51% of those businesses invested more significantly in their finance function.

Do you want to be another of the 81%? I certainly don't but that is exactly where I was heading in 2015 before I made some fundamental changes.

I don't want you to have to go through the same so please, please, please take your own advice and run the ideal finance function for your practice.

3 A TEAM OF A-PLAYERS

People can be amazing, and people can be a right pain. So how do you tell which type of person you are going to get?

Now I can tell you I've hired some right failures in the past! I'm not immune. I've even had to get rid of someone within a week of hiring them before. I've also hired people who have been amazing for a number of years and then things seem to go wrong all of a sudden. Then I've hired people who consistently performed right at the top, continue to grow as individuals and even become better than me in some areas!

Over the past few years, I've got this right more times than wrong and there are some key principles I've learned to achieving this.

Culture is the first step. In my view, this isn't about creating a cult or just writing some words up on your office wall. This is about defining the values you think are important for someone to hold. Values that you live every single day almost without fail. This makes it far easier to hire the people who see the world your way and to hold them accountable for their behaviours.

I've got five that I live by. They are the same for myself and my wife, our family, and our three businesses. They are displayed on our website (go take a look if you want at www.thirveaccountantsacademy.co.uk) for everyone to see.

Our values are:

Do what you say

Nobody likes being let down and we think it's key you don't set unrealistic expectations. Seek to understand the importance of the task and any deadlines and agree realistic timescales and stick to them or communicate early regarding challenges.

Be open and honest

Being a closed book doesn't help anyone. We don't believe work and home are two different lives. Life is just life. By being open and honest about your whole life we can be empathetic to your circumstances and together we can work towards growth and positivity.

Take responsibility

Work-life balance is key and fundamental, we believe, to living a healthy life. We have core hours, but each role also has key outcomes and responsibilities. There will be occasions where flexibility may be needed in order to achieve those outcomes and responsibilities and taking responsibility to act accordingly is key.

Be a team player

As a team, we support and empower each other. There will be occasions where you will need to go outside of the standard scope of your role to help out a colleague. This shouldn't be because we expect it but because you think it's the right thing to do.

Show respect

Respect is everything. It should be a given. It should not come just because of somebody's position but simply because we are all human beings. Being able to be candid with someone about their weaknesses and mistakes when done with love is an absolute sign of respect.

If you have values in your business, do you use them each and every week to ensure you are really living the culture?

We use them for hiring and firing team members, shoutouts for colleagues doing great work, spot rewards for team members, improving team members' behaviours, hiring and firing clients and so much more.

The next level is about creating accountability.

Believe it or not, great people do like being held accountable. They really do, I promise. You see most people would rather be on a losing team than a team that has no idea if it's winning or losing. So why not set standards and then hold people accountable to them?

To do this we need to be able to clearly define what is expected of us and by when. We do this by using a system called scorecards. This is effectively a scoreboard (Excel document) with 3-5 key outcomes the individual needs to achieve for their role. We typically use levels for "keep your job", "good" and "excellent". Typically, we would use things like "number of accounts due within the next 3 months" and "number of client service reviews completed"

With these measures in place, it takes away subjective thoughts on an individual's performance and makes it far more objective. We also work in three pods so you can compare those doing the same role against each other and use it to drive improvements.

Alongside this we use a job description based on the role. Now this is a very specific wording. You see most practices use all-rounders. We certainly used to, and the job role is basically a list of anything and everything they could possibly do. In my view all-rounders rarely exist. We have found the skills required to be a bookkeeper are different to an accountant and different to a management accountant and again different to a client manager. We therefore build each of these key job roles and build job descriptions for each. Staff are then responsible for assessing themselves against their scorecard and their job description to ensure they are performing and progressing. Using the evidence, they capture along the way they can demonstrate their growth and come to you with their progress rather than you having to chase them.

Through these few key acts, we give the staff member control over their own progress and their own career, reducing micro-management.

> "Scorecards can be used to measure the activities that are key to each role being performed successfully removing subjective thoughts on the effectiveness of staff members"

Recruiting is the next step in hiring A players. Now you might wonder why I haven't put this first seeing as surely you must recruit before you put these elements in place. But if you don't have the other areas in place I mentioned earlier then no matter how good your recruitment process is, you'll not be able to maintain the levels of performance. Staff will get frustrated and make mistakes and may even leave.

I believe the quality of candidates in recent years has fallen. With more firms becoming digital, the art of incomplete records accounting is dying and along with it those skills. You see online accounting is great for clients and potentially great for your practice. But in terms of teaching great accountants, it makes the job so much harder. You can't just let a junior loose on a client's online accounting platform because if they make mistakes the client will likely spot it before you do. So, you need to ensure you are finding the very best possible candidates.

So, with this in mind, great recruitment in my view is having deal flow. That means having enough candidates to ensure you have a challenge in selecting the right hire because there are multiple great candidates.

To achieve this we use a 5-step process which looks like this.

Step 1 Run an advert.

Use a platform (such as Indeed or Linkedin) to run your advert but don't follow the crowd. So many job adverts all just look the same. We use business marketing principles here. We ensure we identify the key aspects as to why the candidate would want to work for us and put that right up-front at the start of the advert. Then we add some details about the role, before some testimonials from our existing team and then finally some info about our company. You see the candidate's own needs are far more important to them than yours. Your company is your baby but to them, it's just another company. So ensure you explain to them what is in it for them first.

Step 2 Experience check.

If you are hiring for a role that does require a degree of experience, then do a really quick CV scan to see they have the required experience. It might be they must have worked in practice for 5 years (to get to know the logistics of constantly changing clients you are working on) then check that this exists.

Don't waste time reading all through their CV, it's just their sales letter really. Get what you need from it which is the list of relevant experience.

Step 3 Skills review.

We use a practical skills test that we send to all candidates that get to this stage. We have this in place due to the lack of quality we are experiencing from candidates in terms of their accounting skills. The test is designed to be done without interview pressures and to actually test their ability to apply their skills in a practical manner. We find many fail at this stage. I'm talking a 70% failure rate. It's not a complex test but it is role relevant and just tests around 6-10 relevant things from a typical week in their role that they may come across.

Step 4 Culture interview.

By this stage we have got candidates coming through who we know have relevant experience and have demonstrated being able to do the basics for the role. Now we do a quick 15-minute interview focused on culture fit. It's a brief fairly informal chat with some questions designed to reveal their own underlying beliefs to see if they align. This interview is often done by someone from the team who really gets the culture. It's a very light-hearted interview. You want the candidate to feel comfortable and to allow their real character to come through, not the polished interview-ready version of them. The job of the interviewer here is to disarm the candidate and allow them to be the real them.

As you do this, you'll start to see patterns of those who really align to your values and see the world the way you do. About 50% will fall out at this stage.

Step 5 Final interview

By this stage, you should be down to less than 10 candidates. We typically, therefore, start with around 500 candidates completing the initial application. At this stage of the process though you are looking to make a great hire. If you cannot be confident of that then the alternative option is you do not hire and you repeat the entire process. We have done this before a few times. We use this stage to combine a couple of interview techniques. We use real-world scenarios to test how they would act in those situations. We explain the situation and then get them to repeat it back to ensure they understand. Then we throw in the question and give them space and time to think.

We then also use role play to test candidates, particularly in high communication roles such as managers, receptionists, and advisory roles. This interview is trying to replicate a typical day in that role. If your new receptionist cannot handle a difficult demanding phone call in an interview what chance have they got once they are actually doing the job?

Deal flow is key to a great recruitment process. We typically get 500+ applications for a vacancy and with that many, a clear process to get through to the highest quality candidates quickly is needed.

Ensure you use different staff members in the actual recruitment process if you can. Some aspects of this process are still subjective, and you need to not rely on one person's judgement.

4 THE "SAT-NAV" SALES PROCESS

Sales seems like such a dirty word to many accountants. However, we must become great at sales. We really must!

You see once you own a practice you aren't an accountant anymore. You are the HR department, finance department, operations department and the sales and marketing department too.

Let's face it nobody else is going to do the sales unless you do.

There are loads of terrific books and training courses available on sales. I've read, watched and consumed many of them. I've formed one main opinion and that is the best way to do sales is to work out who you really help, what their pain points are, how you help them overcome them and how they will feel afterwards.

So rather than make sales dirty we have a process that we use that we teach all of our team that makes sales far easier. It is designed to follow a clear process that helps the client see the real value of what you can offer.

In order for the process to work you have to understand that you must position yourself as the expert. You need to take control of the conversation and guide the client towards the outcome. To do that you have to recognise and understand how a client could improve their outcomes by working with you.

Here is how the process works.

Imagine you are lost. The greatest tool here would be a "sat-nav" system which would work like this

1 - Where are you at now? - You need to understand where the client is right now. Be that turnover, profits, time spent working, how they feel and more.

2 - Where are you trying to get to? - You then need to understand the destination they are trying to reach. It's usually an improvement on one of the original factors. You can sometimes switch this part to first and part 1 to second if you are struggling to get the client to open up.

3 - Why can't they get there? - You then need to understand why they are lost. What is actually stopping them from getting from where they are now to where they want to be?

4 - When do they need to arrive? - You need to understand if there is any level of urgency. Is there some degree of imminent issue or is this a longer-term focus?

5 - What is the solution? - You now have to take all of this and your expert understanding and present to them the only solution that will work. This is your duty to you and to the client.

It goes something like this

Accountant (A) – "So can you tell me about where you are at right now? The size of the business, your earnings, the hours you work"

Potential Client (PC) – "Yes so the business is around £300k turnover right now, I take about £3k a month, if it's available, and I'd say I'm working about 60 hours a week"

A – "Great, thanks for that. Would you say you are happy?"

PC – "Great question. Am I happy? If I'm being honest then no. I'd much prefer to work less hours and ideally, I'd like to be able to take home £5k a month".

A – "Less hours? Do you have a number in mind?"

PC – "Ah yes so at first I'd like to work normal hours so around 40 a week but longer term maybe 25-30?"

A – "OK so you said you also want to increase your earnings to £5k a month. Do you know what the business needs to look like to make these two factors a reality? What I mean is what turnover would you need to hit in order to allow you to work less hours, by hiring additional help and to also pay you the additional £2k a month?"

PC – "I don't know the exact figure no. At a guess, I'd say I'd need an assistant at say £25k plus the additional £24k a year. That's at least £50k before any additional other costs so maybe £100k, I don't know".

A – "Thanks for that. I think it would be useful to sit down if we work together and build a strategic plan for the next few years to see what this really needs to look like."

PC – "That sounds like a good idea."

A – "So you've told me about these goals of working less hours and earning more. Why don't you think you are there right now? What's been stopping you?"

PC – "Hmmm, well, what's been stopping me. Me! Seriously me, I've never run a company of this size before and I feel a bit out of my depth. Then there is managing the team, I don't feel I'm so great at that. Then I don't have up-to-date accounts, so I don't know if the new things I'm trying are having the best results for the business and me."

A - "Thanks for letting me into that. It's really useful. Many of us feel like we don't know what we are doing when running a company, you aren't alone. I'd like to say it gets easier and it does but the challenges don't stop, you just get more experienced in dealing with them. We have some great tools that can help you with this though such as our quarterly planning, management reports and coaching services. I'll consider these when we build the proposal later."

"Just considering the time it would take by what date would you like to achieve your goals? Is there any impending deadline?"

PC – "No we are all good. Obviously, I'd like it to get better sooner rather than later but we are good. The next 1-2 years would be good."

A – "Great that time scale seems reasonable and we can certainly help you over that timeframe to move towards those goals."

"So, now you have given me all this info let me just confirm it back to you to ensure I've understood:

- Right now you are at £300k turnover, you take about £3k a month from the company and you work about 60 hours a week.
- You'd like to earn more like £5k a month and you'd like to reduce your working hours at least to 40 but ideally 30 or less by hiring an assistant
- To achieve these goals, you think you need to increase sales by at least £100k but this needs more clarity, maybe a strategic planning session
- You are trying things to improve the business but the financials aren't up to date to be able to give you the clarity you want and need to see if it's working
- You aren't in a rush to get the results and realise it could take a few years to get real progress

"Have I got that right?"

PC – "Yes that sounds correct"

A – "Great, so given all this info I'm now going to pull together a proposal for you, that matches exactly what you told me you need. I've used my knowledge and experience of working with other business owners just like you and helping them make changes just like you want to achieve to put together a blend of services that will really help you go to where you want to go and then can grow with you as you go beyond those levels too. Sound good?"

PC – "Sounds good"

Now you build the proposal that gives them exactly what they need to get to where they want to get to from where they are right now.

> The best way to get great at this sales process or for that matter any new process is through practice.
>
> We always recommend role-play. It might seem daunting but it's so effective and once you have done it for a few minutes all the nerves are gone.

5 EFFECTIVE CLIENT REVIEWS

In my view, the next step in running a thriving accounting practice is to take this great setup you now have for gaining new clients and to apply it to keeping and retaining the top clients you already have.

So, you have taken steps to get the financial control in place and that allowed you to have a great team who believe in what you believe in and you now know how to sell to potential new clients.

However, you likely already have some really great clients, or at least clients with the potential to be great! You though, need to be able to unlock that potential.

In my view, that comes through the number one thing that clients tell us we as accountants are bad at, and that is clear communication! It's no secret that the number one reason clients change accountants is due to a lack of clear communication. You might think it's not you and it's them, but communication is more about what is received than what is delivered.

So, you need to be able to tackle this issue head on. In our practice we use a process that is remarkably similar to our sat-nav sales process to achieve this. The process is focused on understanding your client. What it is that they are trying to achieve and what it is that is stopping them?

By simply applying the sat-nav sales process to your existing clients, you can ensure they feel heard. You build that relationship with them and you become a partner for them to achieve what they thought was never possible.

There are a few ways to go about this. Firstly, listen to the questions that your clients are asking. Your whole team needs to be listening out for calls for help. They usually show up a little like moaning or complaints. This is the client giving you a signal to help them. Something like "Xero is so frustrating I don't know how to use it to see my accounts and when I do there's just numbers everywhere I just can't work it out". It would be so easy to just brush this off as a moaning client, but actually it's a request for help. I know that we find numbers easy to understand but the reality is clients don't. For this reason, we do very visual management reporting. For this client getting them to upgrade to a monthly management report either with video analysis or a meeting would really help them. So, take them through the sat-nav sales process and understand their pain and help them overcome it.

Secondly, be regular when reviewing clients. We plan that every client gets a review at least annually. We have this as a key part of a team member's role. That is a deep review of a client their goals and ambitions versus where they are now.

The third area is seeing shifts in their business, hiring more people, making more sales, struggling with cash flow and more. You need to have processes that allow these to be captured and actioned. There is more work involved if transaction numbers increase or if the number of staff increases and these need to be spotted and a new proposal sent and accepted without delay.

> Accountants are one of the most trusted people. However, our lack of communication skills puts blockages in the way. My best tip is to stop overthinking things and be there to support and help.

6 BEING EVERYTHING TO EVERYONE

I'm not one of these guys who when asked the question "What would you do if you started again?" says I'd go right after my ideal market from day one!

It's such a cliche answer and in my view, it shows how far someone has come that they have lost touch with the reality of where they came from. In those early days, there is one goal and one goal only. That goal is to generate enough income to pay yourself so you can pay your bills. That's it. That does mean attracting every client, some good, some ok and even some bad. This usually shows up as some good effective marketing attracting your practice more and more clients and keeping you very busy. However, your very success becomes your own downfall.

This usually creates a practice that is reactive to each and every client's individual needs and whilst saying you customise your service to each client, actually doing that for a larger scalable practice is near on impossible. We then keep making excuses for ourselves and we keep hold of existing bad clients in the hope that they change, and we keep bringing in more bad clients on the basis that we have learned how to change them to good.

If you take it back to Business 101 then the best guidance is DO NOT try to be everything to everyone as otherwise, you'll end up being nothing to nobody. I made the exact same mistake with my practice. The mistake though wasn't attracting all these clients in the first place as they did allow me to pay my bills. The mistake was not making the decision sooner to focus on who I could really help.

So, they call it a niche but, in my view, it's just being clear on who you really help. It could be a specific sector, or it could be people with particular hobbies or interests, or it could be female business owners or something else. It needs though to be clear to the business owners you are targeting for them to see how you can really make a big impact in their lives and become their trusted advisor.

If you were going to niche today, who would you focus on and why?

> Keeping measuring my success based on the number of clients we had was one of my worse decisions. I was focused on the wrong thing and it allowed me to fool myself that I was doing better than I was. Focusing on better metrics such as average monthly fees per client, monthly free cashflow and others was a much better decision.

7 HAVING FINANCIAL CLARITY

You may think I'm absolutely mad for deciding to tackle financial clarity in a book aimed at financial experts! What accountant actually needs to know about financial control and financial clarity?

Actually, the secret is, we all do. It's not that we don't know it, it's that we don't take our own advice. Come on, we all know the mechanic who does amazing work on people's cars but drives around in a complete wreck.

So, in my view, financial clarity is the ability to be able to see and understand our financial performance. That means having a budget that is well thought out and so that we can track performance against, having KPIs that measure key areas, producing management accounts and reporting our results. Then taking a look at how we can improve, have a cash flow forecast at least the next 3 months and provision funds for VAT, tax and unexpected bills.

None of that was surprising or unexpected, I'm sure. However, how many of us as accountants can truly say we do all of these for our own practice? We certainly didn't. We were bookkeeping just to do VAT returns and didn't have any regular reporting. A big change for us was the moment we decided that we should treat our own practice like our number one client.

We will take our practice through the sat-nav sales process and identify exactly what we believe our practice would want and need from us as a client. We then simply ensure we deliver every possible service to our practice just like it was a client. You might think I'm mad but I produce management reports and present them to my wife (my fellow director) and we scrutinise them. Why wouldn't we?

If you cannot sell each and every service to yourself when it's effectively free (or at least at cost price) then what chance have you got in convincing clients to take them on?

So, it's time to review your practice like it was a client coming to see you for some great advice. You can roleplay the sales meeting and go through exactly what would be best for the "client" and start delivering it ASAP.

Trust me, it will be one of the best decisions you ever make. You can thank me later!

> We as accountants are special. We truly are. We have the advantage of being able to speak the language of business (accounting). However, we rarely use it to our advantage. To do is the day when you should take advantage of that "cheat code" and start delivering every service you offer to your own practice.

8 CREATING FINANCIAL FREEDOM

Financial freedom always seems hard to define. However, in my view it is having the ability to do what you want, with who you want to do it with, when you want to do it.

So, my question to you is; What do you want to be able to do, who with and when?

Then, what is the actual chance of you being able to do that, as often as you want?

For me it's to be able to spend quality time with my family without the distraction of work every weekend but also by going abroad in the sun at least two but ideally four times a year.

I've managed to achieve this the last few years and have visited Spain, The Canary Islands, Egypt, Tunisia, Majorca, Ireland and France.

Now yours might be similar or it might be completely different. It doesn't really matter, to be honest. The point is to take the time to decide what financial freedom means to you so you can then make active plans and steps towards it being a reality.

Most of the time when we as practice owners create a plan, we tend to take the last year and try and do a bit better. This, however, isn't really the best method. If all we try to be is a bit better than last the year, then how are we really seizing the opportunities that could be coming our way? If we cast our thoughts further in the future (maybe 5 or 10 years) and create the business that would give us the life we want then we can scale that back to what it needs to look like in 12 months' time. I started doing this process back in 2019 and it has really accelerated my business and personal growth. This process in my experience creates a far better way of actually achieving financial freedom.

We use the method of

Financial Results

Key Performance Indicators (KPI)

Activities

Great Team

What this means is (working from bottom to top) if you put a great team in place, they then do the right activities which drive the KPI's which in turn brings the financial results.

Whilst we want to achieve the top result in the table, the financial results, we have to have the rest of the table in place first. That's the KPI's in place to be able to help us predict in advance if these will happen. Prior to that we must ensure we are doing the right activities in the right way and prior to that to do those activities we need to have an amazing team in place.

All of this running smoothly means you manage to achieve financial freedom.

> Napolean Hill arguably wrote the best business book of all time, Think and Grow Rich. Notice it doesn't say do or work hard or be mean or be nice it says THINK. People are great doers. We are great at working hard. We don't, however put time aside to think. You need to really value this process and thank me later. It's one of the biggest catalysts in changing my life for the better.

So, many people focus on having a great time when they retire. However, there are no guarantees any of us will even make it to retirement and there are no guarantees we can sell our practice for a great price to be able to afford to have a great retirement.

For this reason, I decided to focus on not trying to get to a destination where I sell and make decent money one day but to focus on enjoying the journey at the same time.

By enjoying the journey I don't have regrets, I don't have an "I'll do that someday approach", I'm far more intentional and do things right now because I want to and because I can.

I'm sure you are thinking that's alright for you and where you got to but

I'm not there yet. But neither was I. I had to start somewhere and changing my mindset was the first step. I wanted to have a life that I deemed successful and so we started making plans for much more success right now.

Things like being able to have weekends off, then to be able to take holidays, then to take holidays without any calls about work, then working no evenings, then having Fridays off, then to not doing technical work (which when I do actually do some causes me and the team stress), then by taking multiple holidays per year and I just keep going.

It was broken down into small chunks but, all focused on a longer-term goal where I became unimportant to the day-to-day operations. It was scary as I liked to be thought of as important, but the truth is, the less important I got and the more boring the business became, through operating more smoothly, the more money we made.

Now I'm not pretending that sometimes I don't have to work an evening, or a Friday, or get a call while I'm on holiday, things still go wrong but the point is they are few and far between. It's not some pipedream. I'm a normal accountant just like you and yet, I've managed to achieve having the life I really wanted, so what's stopping you?

What's even better is that I genuinely want our industry to improve and get even better so I'm going to be sharing my journey of what's worked and what hasn't to get me to where I am and to where I'm going, all so you don't have to make the same mistakes.

I won't pretend that there are no hard decisions and some hard work to be put in but if I honestly look at my life now versus where I was back in 2015 it's far better and it's because I decided to do something about it.

> Believe it or not, I'm not special. I'm a human being who happens to be an accountant just like you. However, I chose to no longer accept the average life I had and to go on a journey to financial freedom, one where the journey is equally as rewarding as the destination. You can do it too.

9 NEXT STEPS

Firstly, thanks so much for taking the time to read through this book. It's much appreciated.

You need to become a better practice owner to be able to get a better practice. There are 3 foundations to achieving better financial results and they are

Financial Control Financial Clarity Financial Freedom

You must put in the work and do the boring hard work that many others won't. You don't want to be average, so stop doing the same things that the average person does (or doesn't do). Break the norm and be different.

I'd love to be able to give you something back.

I'm active on social media, Facebook mainly and you can find me and my group for thriving accountants at these links or by scanning the QR codes.

> Now is the time for you to take control of your journey from surviving to thriving. Take the time now to install financial control, gain financial clarity and achieve financial freedom

Thriving Accountants Community on Facebook

https://tinyurl.com/TAA-FB

I have a scorecard you can take to see how you compare to the areas I consider are essential to a thriving accounting practice.

Simply head over to our website using the link below or scan the QR code below

Take the scorecard

https://tinyurl.com/TAA-SC

ABOUT THE AUTHOR

Ian Morgan is an accountant, business owner, podcast host, husband and dad to four children.

Ian started his self-employed journey in 2010 joining the bookkeeping and payroll firm founded by his wife, Sam, around 5 years earlier as an income source that worked around starting our family. Sam had built something that provided a small but steady income that really worked around having children.

Early success came through being a traditional accounting practice mainly filing tax returns which saw Ian nominated for accounting technician of the year for which he came runner-up but it soon became a difficult beast to tame. The next six years continued to follow a very similar pattern with online marketing continuing to bring in clients each and every month.

Since 2016 Ian has been on a journey of self-discovery and education. He dropped his ego (the one that most entrepreneurs seem to have), the one where he felt he always knew best and set about looking for what he didn't know and how he could be better in his business and personal life, even if just by 1-2%. That led him to undertake various courses, training and masterminds covering everything from sales and marketing to financial management, culture development, and team building.

Ian reads regularly, mainly business and education books with his favourites being Take Your Shot by Robin Waite, Traction by Gino Wickman and Start with Why by Simon Sinek. Ian also loves listening to podcasts (even if the kids aren't such a fan on the school run) such as Diary of a CEO and The High Performance Podcast.

Over the years since the practice has continued to go from strength to strength and the measure of success has changed. Where it always used to be the number of clients it is now, profit, monthly cash flow and average fee per client.

Ian is now the Strategic Development Director of his accountancy business, MBS Accountants, and is extracted so much that he chooses to work rather than needing to work.

With this being the case Ian has started to follow his real passion, which is helping business owners to change their lives from surviving to thriving through the successes and the failures he has had along his journey.

He started with coaching clients and helping them to really transition their business before starting to coach owners of accounting practices before moving into creating masterminds for accounting practice owners teaching everything he has learned along the way.

For Ian, this level of success hasn't come about without a number of failings and learnings along the way, but he is a firm believer that you either win or you learn, not that you win or you lose.

Printed in Great Britain
by Amazon